CompTIA Cloud+

Certification Study Guide
Exam CV0-001

Table of Contents

4

Introduction

The CompTIA Cloud+ (Exam CV0-001) exam can be tough, especially with poor preparation for it. It is essential for you to read the right materials as you prepare for this exam. This book explores the topics which you should read so as to tackle this exam. It is the best book to prepare you for this exam. Read it, and you will never regret it!

Chapter 1- Cloud Models

Cloud providers usually market and sell everything in the form of a service, and the type of service one subscribes to will be named for the highest level of technology which may be provided. If the computing and the storage are of the highest level, the client will subscribe for Infrastructure as a Service (IaaS). If there are applications which are involved, they will have to purchase the Software as a Service (SaaS).

Let us discuss the types of services which cloud providers offer to their subscribers:

Infrastructure as a Service

If a company needs extra network capacity such as storage, processing power, and networking services such as firewalls, but they don't have funds for buying more network hardware, then IaaS becomes the best option. The Infrastructure as a Service functions more like a utility, since the client is expected to pay for what they will be using. The IaaS requires the highest network management expertise from its client, as the client will provide and manage the software.

IaaS refers to the provision of the capability to a consumer to provision the processing, networks, storage, and other fundamental computing resources in an environment where the consumer has the capability to deploy and run any software, including operating systems and other applications.

Software as a Service (SaaS)

The Software as a Service forms the highest service of the three levels of services which are available. It deals with the work of managing software together with its deployment, having both the platform and the infrastructure. Google Docs and Microsoft Office 365 use this type of service. The main benefit associated with this model is that it helps in cutting costs for the process of software ownership and management. The client is allowed to sign up for the subscriptions to use software, and they are able to renew the subscription as they need.

The SaaS refers to the providing consumers with the capability to use the applications of the provider which are running on the cloud infrastructure.

Platform as a Service

This works by adding a layer to the IaaS which has the software development tools such as runtime environments. This platform is very useful to software developers, as the vendor usually takes the responsibility of managing the hardware platforms on behalf of the developer. The developer in turn concentrates on the development and delivery of high quality applications. The best PaaS solution is the one which allows the client to export the developed programs and then run them in an environment other than the one in which the development was done. Examples of PaaS include Microsoft Azure and Google App Engine.

PaaS refers to providing capability to a consumer to deploy apps into the cloud infrastructure, in which the applications can be consumer-created or acquired by use of programming languages, services, libraries, and the tools which are supported by the provider.

Business Process as a Service

This occurs whereby the services of the cloud model goes beyond the provision of IT services to the provision of business-related services. In this type of cloud mode, the steps involved in carrying out business tasks are monitored by use of any of the available cloud models. This helps the one in charge of monitoring the business activities to come up with feedback in terms of the progress of these activities. With this, it will be possible for the business to come up with measures which can help them to optimize their business processes. This is because they will be able to know the processes which are about to fail and then take any necessary measures so as to combat it.

Communication as a Service

This type of cloud model allows a consumer to utilize VoIP, PBX, VPNs, and Unified Communications at the Enterprise level without having to incur the cost of purchasing, hosting, and then managing the infrastructure. A service provider is available for the management and running of such services. Due to this, the client also enjoys a great reduction in cost, as they don't have to hire any qualified or trained personnel for management of the services.

Monitoring as a Service (MaaS)

This model is an emerging piece of Cloud jigsaw as well as an integral one for future. In a similar manner that businesses realized that the infrastructure and the key applications they use require monitoring tools which would ensure that there is a proactive elimination of downtime risks, the Monitoring as a Service offers the option for offloading a large majority of such costs by having this run like a service rather than having a fully equipped in-house tool. Once you log onto some thin client or a central web-based dashboard that has been hosted by a service provider, the consumer will be in a position to monitor the status of key applications which have been deployed regardless of their location. The other advantages associated with this type of cloud setup include an easy set up, purchasing the process, and this model could be a pay as you use model so as to de-risk the applications which are initially migrated to your Cloud.

Anything as a Service (XaaS)

This cloud model involves delivery of IT as a Service via a hybrid Cloud computing, and this is a reference to one or more of Infrastructure as a Service (IaaS), Software as a Service (SaaS), Platform as a Service (PaaS), monitoring as a service (Maas), or communications as a service (CaaS). This cloud model is quickly coming up as a term which is readily recognized as services which were previously separated on private or public Clouds which are becoming more transparent and integrated.

Database as a Service (DBaaS)

In this type of cloud model, a software system is used for supporting the database operations. With this, the majority of the consumers will be in a position to enjoy the provision of database services. In this case, the instances must be monitored so that it can be possible to measure the level of services which the consumers are getting.

Cloud Computing Deployment Models

The cloud hosting deployment models refers to the exact type of cloud environment which are mainly differentiated by size, proprietorship, and access. It is responsible for telling the purpose and nature of a cloud. The majority of organizations are readily willing to implement a cloud since it will reduce the capital expenditure as well as control the operating cost. For you to know the deployment model which matches the website requirements, you should first understand the four deployment models which are provided. Let us discuss these:

Public Cloud

This is a cloud hosting whereby the cloud services which are provided are offered via a network that is open to the public. This model is a true representation of cloud hosting; in this the service provider renders services and infrastructure to many clients. There is no mechanism for differentiating the customers and controlling access to the resources. When viewed from a technical point, there may be no great difference between a private and a public cloud. The only difference we can talk of is the level of security which is provided in a private cloud.

A public cloud is the best for catering any business requirements which need management of a load and services which are being used by many users. It is a very economical model due to its reduced cost of management. The charges may be based on pay per user or even free. The costs of the cloud are shared among the users, meaning that they will enjoy the benefits of large scale. A good example of public cloud storage is Google.

Private Cloud

Some businesses refer to this as an "internal cloud." This is a cloud model which is implemented so that it can be a secure environment safeguarded by use of a firewall. The maintenance of this firewall is left in the hands of an IT department belonging to a corporation.

Note that only the authorized users are granted access to a private cloud, meaning that the organization will exercise a greater level of control over the data they own. The computers may be hosted either internally or externally, and the resources must be offered from a specific pool and then into the private cloud.

Businesses with unforeseen or dynamic needs, security alarms, mission critical assignments, uptime requirements, or management demands are good to adopt a private cloud. However, it is good for you to note that vulnerabilities may occur in a cloud in cases of calamities, disasters, or in case a theft of data occurs.

Hybrid Cloud

This is an integrated cloud computing environment. It can be made up of either two or more cloud servers, that is, public, private, or community clouds which are bound together while remaining individual entities. The hybrid cloud hosting is beneficial to multiple deployments. This type of cloud is capable of overcoming isolations and boundaries in the cloud, making it difficult for us to classify it as either public, private, or a community cloud. With a hybrid cloud, the user is allowed to increase the capacity as well as the capability by use of aggregation, customization, or assimilation with another cloud service or package. The provision and management of the available resources is done by external providers or in-house.

Resources which are non-critical, such as development and the test workloads, may be housed in a public cloud which belongs to some third-party provider. Workloads which are critical or are sensitive should be housed internally. Businesses which have a focus on security and the demand for having a unique presence should implement a hybrid cloud as the most effective business strategy. If they face demand spikes, any additional resources which are required by the particular application may be accessed from a public cloud. This process is known as cloud bursting, and the hybrid cloud provides this.

Community Cloud

This is a cloud hosting whereby the setup is shared mutually between many organizations which belong to some particular community, that is, banks and other trading firms. It involves a multi-tenant setup which is shared among several organizations which belong to a particular group with similar computing requirements. The members of the community usually share similar performance, privacy, and security concerns. Their main intention is to attain their business objectives. The management of the community cloud can be done either or by some third party provider. The hosting can be done externally or internally.

The specific organizations which belong to the community usually share the various costs, hence, providing them with a saving capacity in the community cloud. This type of cloud is suitable for organizations and businesses which work on joint tenders, ventures, or research which needs a centralized cloud computing capability for management, building, and implementation of similar projects.

The majority of organizations have known that cloud hosting has much potential. For you to emerge the best among the rest, choosing the right type of the cloud hosting is essential. This means that you should know your business and then analyse the demands. After selection of the necessary type of the cloud hosting, it will be easy for you to achieve your business goals very easily, and channelize all your efforts towards taking the strategic steps which will help the business to succeed.

Security differences between models

1. Multitenancy Issues

The workloads from the different clients may be on a similar system and a flaw in the implementation may compromise the security. The "multi-tenant" nature of a cloud means that the security incidents may originate from another customer in the cloud provider. There is a need for data to be protected from the other cloud consumers as well as from the cloud provider as well.

With multitenant applications, there will be an assurance that the individual tenants are not granted access so as to be able to change the configuration and data of the application on their own. However, each tenant will be allowed to make changes to the user interface of the application so that they experience a different look and feel.

The problem comes in the development of the multitenant applications as opposed to the development of single tenant applications as a result of the complexity which is involved. A multitenant app should be able to support the use of different resources by the different users.

2. Laws and regulations

The consumer is tasked with the responsibility of compliance. A service level agreement (SLA) usually defines the terms related to the functionality and the performance validation depending on the delivery method which is chosen. A high availability and the minimal downtimes are usually desired, and any other model chosen requires fitting business processes for which the implementation is being done.

Service orchestration refers to the composition of the system components which support the activities of the cloud provider in coordination, arrangement, and management of the computing resources so as to offer secure cloud services to the cloud consumers.

3. Metering

Cloud systems automatically control and optimize the resource usage by leveraging some metering capability at a level of abstraction which is appropriate to the type of service such as storage, bandwidth, processing, or the active user accounts.

The usage of resources can be controlled, monitored, and reported so as to provide transparency for the provider and the consumer of the service. Metering also helps to perform billing for the services which a particular user has used in the cloud.

4. Network Isolation

It is possible that there will be a malicious cloud tenant. Such a tenant can take advantage of side channel attacks based on cache-based and network-based channels for the purpose of gaining a co-residence virtual machine of a victim tenant. This calls for us to employ the technique of network isolation.

5. Data Segregation

Cloud computing provides organizations the ability to run their workloads and to manage their data anywhere without having significant computing resources in their business. Cloud providers make use of multi-tenant infrastructures so as to maximize their cost-effectiveness, so the businesses must implement data separation and the relocation issues in an increasingly complex international legal as well as a political landscape.

The businesses should consider two major factors regarding data separation in a public cloud, which includes tenancy and relocation. The cloud computing is dependent on the underlying virtualization technology which shares the computing resources.

Orchestration platforms

Service orchestration refers to the composition of the system components which support the activities of the cloud provider in coordination, arrangement, and management of the computing resources so as to offer secure cloud services to the cloud consumers.

Terms and Characteristics of the Cloud

The following are the common terms and characteristics of the cloud:

1. Elasticity

    This refers to the capability to scale up the resources as required. Mostly, the clients are able to get more resources instantly with no need to purchase, install, and then configure a new hardware. It is also possible for elasticity to work backwards, whereby if you need fewer resources, the client will be in a position to scale down and then pay less with no need to sell the hardware. Elasticity is one of the characteristics of the cloud.

    With elasticity, the capabilities can be provisioned and then released elastically, in other cases automatically, so as to scale outward and inward rapidly in response to the demand. In the case of a consumer, the capabilities for provisioning usually seem to be unlimited, and they can be appropriated in the right quantity during any time.

2. On-demand self serve/just in time service- With the on-demand model, the users are able to access the additional storage, processing, and other capabilities automatically with no need for intervention from a service provider.

    The true key for this is that the human interaction from a service provider doesn't have to be needed.

3. Pay-as-you-grow- the subscriptions with a built-in elasticity are known as the pay-as-you-grow models. The key to these is that they may require upfront costs

and the payment for the services is done as they are used.

4. Chargeback- This decentralizes the IT costs and then allocates them to the ones incurring them. Nearly everyone has gone through the misfortune of working with an organization in which all the expenses are unfairly charged to a single account and the chargeback is the opposite of that. This feature helps to solve this problem.

5. Ubiquitous access- This means that cloud capabilities is accessible over the network by different types of clients, such as workstations, laptops, and mobile phones, by use of common access software such as the web browsers. Users are offered the ability to get the data that they need, when they need it, and how they need it. Note that all users are given the same level of access regardless of the location which they are in.

6. Metering resource pooling- this is closely related to virtualization, with the resource pooling the resources of the provider which are seen as being one large pool which can be divided up among the clients as it is needed. Generally, the clients do not have control or knowledge over exact physical location whereby the resources provided should be located, but they should be in a position to access the additional resources as it is needed.

7. Cloud bursting- the premise which is behind the cloud bursting is the one which when the demand has become too great for the private cloud, some of the available load can be seamlessly moved to some public cloud.

8. Rapid deployment- this forms one of principle promises of cloud computing together with cost savings, scalability, and empowerment. The deployment models

24

for this are the ones we have already discussed, that is, public, community, private, and hybrid.

9. Automation- since there is no human interaction on the provider's part, there it exists five key areas in which the automation comes to play. These include the automated provisioning of the computing and storage resources, the automated deployment of the related components, the automated tools, the automated reporting of any problems and outages, and the automated vulnerability monitoring tools.

Concepts in Object Storage

The object storage involves the storage of files and other types of data. The access to such data is done by use of APIs. A web interface can also be used for accessing the object storage. The following are some of the concepts in object storage:

1. Object ID- this is a unique identifier for each piece of data as well as the associated metadata making up the object.

2. Metadata- this refers to the data which describes other data, and it is seen as a set of attributes or the data about data.

3. Access control- this is a security component in the cloud which depends on a functional requirement. In some other cases, it is known as Identity Control.

4. Data/blob- means a "binary large object." It refers to binary data collected together and then stored like a single entity.

5. Extensive Metadata- this is similar to metadata, as it used for the description of data, but it is used for proprietary purposes. It is dependent on the entity which it is describing, such as the service provider, or identity provider.

6. Replicas- replicas are used for decreasing risk and increasing the availability.

7. Policies- these work in a similar manner to metadata, but they have to do with issues relating to security.

On-premise vs. Off-premise Hosting

A cloud system can be hosted on the premises of a cloud customer or a third party may task with hosting, and this is determined by the kind of deployment model which is being provided. Different deployments usually come with tradeoffs in the number of customers who have access to the resources and the costs of maintaining a datacenter. A cloud provider may have access to the large quantities of the resources of the other parties which may raise some security concerns.

Chapter 2- Virtualization

Virtualization refers to making a virtual version of a server, a desktop, or an operating system. With virtualization, the users are able to use a single instance of an application or a resource. In this case, a logical name is assigned to the physical storage, and a pointer is provided to the physical resource once it is demanded.

With virtualization, there exists no one-to-one relationship from a physical server to a logical server. There can be a single physical server hosting the cloud servers virtually for multiple companies, or one may have multiple physical servers which work together as a single logical server. In the case of the end users, they will not be aware of whether they are interacting with a virtual machine or a physical machine, as the handling of this is done behind the scenes.

The main reason behind virtualization is to save money. The cloud service provider is able to enjoy the economies of large scale since they don't have to purchase, install, and configure new hardware whenever new users join the cloud. The clients will also be expected to pay for the services they have used only but not to pay for the hardware costs. The developers will also be provided with a number of environments for use without the need for having to add new hardware.

Hypervisor Types

For virtualization to be implemented in a cloud, a hypervisor, which is also referred to as the virtual machine manager (VMM) is needed. The hypervisor is responsible for allowing the multiple operating systems to use a similar host, and it is tasked with the management of the allocation of the physical resources to the virtual operating systems.

The following are the two main types of hypervisors:

- Bare metal (Type I)
- Operating System dependent (Type II)

Type I

In type I, the hypervisor will always run regardless of the operating system. It always boots up before the operating system, and it will form the OS for the physical machine. This type of virtualization is commonly used on the server side, since the hypervisor has very low hardware requirements for supporting the functions it needs.

The type I hypervisor is well for its better performance when compared to the type 2 hypervisor. This is because there is no involvement of a host OS, and your system will be dedicated so that it can support virtualization. The running of virtual operating systems is done within the hypervisor, and the guest or the virtual operating systems all independently from one another.

Type II

This type of hypervisor is very reliable on operating. It cannot boot unless the operating system is up and running. This is because it needs the operating system so as to run. Most people refer to it as the "host OS." This type of hypervisor is highly used in the client-side of the virtualization environments. In this case, multiple operating systems are under management, as opposed to the management of a single server.

A good example of this is a Windows user who needs to use Linux simultaneously with Windows. The user may achieve this by installing a hypervisor, and then install Linux in the hypervisor. The two operating systems will then be run simultaneously and independently. The Type 2 hypervisor has a disadvantage in that the hosts OS will consume system resources such as memory and processor time and in case the host operating system encounters a failure, then the guest operating system will also fail!

For exam purposes, remember that the Type I hypervisor offers a better performance and scalability as opposed to the Type II hypervisor.
In the case of system requirements, you should always remember that the running of multiple operating systems on a single system will require more resources as compared to running a single operating system, meaning that you have to equip your system very well in terms of memory, CPU, network performance, and the hard drive space. This should be the case with the Type 2 hypervisor systems, since they have one operating system running on top of another operating system.

Since the host operating system will need resources, it means that it will be competing with the OS running on the virtual machine for the same. All hosts which are running on the cluster must be homogenous. It is recommended that you use static IP addresses, and have enough memory and hard disk space.

Proprietary vs. Open Source

The proprietary and the open solutions are very common. Some solutions, such as xen, feature both the proprietary and the open source solutions. The VMWare ESX is provided for free, but one has to pay for the features. Xen is free as well as open source, while ESX is free, but it is not open source (proprietary). The KVM is free as well as open source, but the Hyper-V for Microsoft is usually free, but it is not open source (proprietary).

Consumer vs. Enterprise use

Both the consumer and the enterprise solutions may be used. The consumer implementations may include embedded deployments, but the consumer implementations shouldn't use enterprise applications because of the excessive overhead. The general rule is that the workstation implementations may be equated to the desktop use, and the cloud use may be equated to infrastructure utilization. The Type I hypervisors are mostly used in enterprises, while the Type II by the consumers.

Virtual Devices and Machines

The process of creating, importing, and then exporting the templates relies on the software which you are using, but there are similar options in most of the software which include the following:

- To export, select File, Export Template.
- To import, select File, Import.

Before the import or the export is done, it is a must for you to agree to the terms of the End User License Agreement (EULA). Each of your virtual desktops will need full network access and when you don't have a template, it will be hard for you to configure each of them. The VM will then create some virtual NIC, and this will make it easy for you to manage the NIC resources.

Guest tools refer to the helpers which are usually installed after the installation of a virtual OS. For the case of VMware for example, one has to install the VMware tools in the workstation menu. A clone refers to a copy of a virtual machine which is in existence. Note that if you make changes to a clone, the parent virtual machine will not be affected. Also, changes made in the parent virtual machine will not be shown in the clone.

A snapshot refers to a point-in-time copy of a virtual machine. The File-Level backups are backups of the virtual machines done incrementally. An image backup is an online backup of a virtual machine. The limits for a virtual disk are dependent on the virtual machines which have been used.

A VLAN usually makes it possible and easy for a VNIC to communicate with the other network devices. The Virtual NIC will want values for an IP address, a subnet mask, and a default gateway in a similar manner to what any physical NIC would need.

Virtual Resource Migration

Before you can migrate to some virtual platform, you have to carefully plan for it. Note that all physical servers are not ideal for a good migration. A baseline needs to be created. Over provisioning or under provisioning should be avoided. It is good for you to be aware that migration will involve some downtime, meaning that you should be prepared for a short disruption. With an online migration, your source computer will be kept up during the migration process. With an offline migration, the source computer has to be put offline during the migration process.

Some of the reasons as to why we may choose migration include performance issues, upgrading existing systems, testing needs and a better utilization of resources. The common types of migration include:

- Physical to Virtual (P2V)- migration from physical to virtual
- Virtual to Virtual (V2V)- migration from one virtual machine to another
- Virtual to Physical (V2P) - migration from virtual to physical

Virtual Components

There are some terms which are related to virtualization. These include the following:

1. Virtual NIC- this allows for interaction with the other devices on the network, and it has a MAC/IP address as well as the network configuration settings.

2. Virtual HBA- this enables one physical Fibre Channel HBA port to work as many logical ports, each having its own identity.

3. Virtual Router- this is for software only, and it works like a hardware router.

4. Shared memory- the settings for the virtual memory can be changed as required. The configuration of this can be done dynamically or as a static value.

5. Shared storage- this can be implemented on NAS, SAN, etc. The virtual machine will only see the physical disk.

6. Virtual CPU- the installation of this is done on the guest virtual machine, and it will be the same as the physical CPU.

7. Clustered storage- the use of multiple devices can help to improve performance. The alternative to this is Microsoft Clustering Services.

8. NPIV (N port ID Virtualization)- multiple hosts always use the same port ID for physical fiber channel. This is normally used when we need high availability with SAN.

Chapter 3- Infrastructure

For your cloud to work as expected, then the infrastructure must be correctly laid. Let us discuss how one can lay out the right infrastructure in the cloud.

Storage Technologies

In the case of storage technologies in the cloud, there are a number of options. Some of these include the following:

1. Network Attached Storage (NAS)

   This is much easier for one to implement compared to SAN, and it makes use of the TCP/IP. For an individual who is trying to access a file, they will see this as being a file server, and it provides a shared storage.

2. Direct Attached Storage (DAS)

   This provides us with both block level as well as file level access. It is always a dedicated storage which is present in a computer which has been attached to and connected via SATA, IDE, SCSI, etc.

3. Storage Area Network (SAN)

   This is a storage technology which offers a block level access for a high performance. It is a shared storage which allows more than a single computer or user to work simultaneously. HBAs (Host Bus Adapters) are usually needed for communication with SAN, each HBA having a World Wide Name (WWN) which is the same as a MAC address. With the LUN masking, the disks are divided into some logical unit numbers, making the client see it as a disk, but not as a file server. The technique of zoning is the fabric which underlies it all and the Fiber Channel Protocols (FCP) used by the SCSI commands.

The following are the various access protocols which can be used:

- Ethernet

- iSCSI (Internet Small Computer System Interface, makes use of IP for sending of IP commands)

- FCoE (Fiber channel traffic over Ethernet using high-speed of 10GB)

- FC, providing the highest level of performance

In the case of the management of the network, this is determined by the underlying cloud model, as well as the technologies which have been used.

Storage Configuration Concepts

These concepts include the following:

1. Tiring- this is the assigning of different types of data to the different types of storage media so as to save on storage costs. Tiers are usually determined by the performance and cost of media, and the data is ranked by frequency with which it is accessed. Classified as follows:

   - Tier 1- mission-critical
   - Tier 2- business apps
   - Tier 3- not needed on a daily basis
   - Tier 4- archived

2. Disk types- these can be classified into interface types, Spinning/Not Spinning, and access speed. Spinning will translate to the traditional hard drives (HDD) and some moving parts, while not spinning will translate to the solid state drives (SSD). The HDDs make use of magnetic media (with the moving parts), and the SSDs make use of chips which are similar to flash memory (with no moving parts).

3. Raid levels- this is a technique of storing similar data in different places on multiple hard disks. Raid 0 is used to boost the performance of the server and the data in this level is written across multiple disks. The Raid 1 is a fault-tolerant configuration usually referred to as "disk mirroring." The data is copied simultaneously and seamlessly, from one disk to another, so as to create a mirror or a replica. Raid 5 is very common in enterprise NAS devices and business servers. It has a better performance compared to fault tolerance and mirroring. Raid 6 is also common in enterprises. It has an extra parity block compared to Raid 5. Raid 10 combines Raid 1 and 0.

4. File system types- the various types of file systems in the cloud include the following:

   - FAT- means File Allocation Table. It was developed by Microsoft, and holds a file of a maximum of 4GB in size. All operation systems have support for this type of file system.

   - NTFS (New Technology File System)- developed by Microsoft with a more complex structure. Seen as a "journaling" file system since all the records about the operations are kept on the device. Journaling is good for error detection and recovery.

- ZFS- this file system is only supported in the Linux world. It supports files whose size up to 16 Exabyte. Although its performance is not much better, it supports good features such as data corruption protection, volume management concepts, file system combination, transparent compression, and snapshots.

- Ext4- this forms the most common file system in the Linux systems. It has a good performance which makes it possible for the use of different techniques. It's a journaling file system with huge support for hard drives.

- UFS (Unix File System)- this is used in Unix-like operating systems, and it is organized into cylinders.

- VMFS (Virtual Machine File System)- this is a cluster file system which facilitates the storage virtualization for the multiple installations of a VMware ESX Server, which is a hypervisor which partitions the physical servers to get multiple virtual machines.

Holding all other factors constant, the SSD drives perform faster than the HDD ones, and they don't go through fragmentation issues. However, they are more expensive. The available types of interfaces can be IDE/ATA (PATA/SATA), Fiber Channel (FC) or SCSI. The measurement of access speed is done in terms of the access time. The seek refers to the amount of time that it takes for you to find what you have been looking for. Latency refers to the delay in time. Both seek and latency is affected by the spin time.

Storage Provisioning

The Logical Unit Numbers (LUNs) are unique identifiers which came from the SCSI world. The SAN and NAS are the targets holding up to 8 devices. With LUN masking and zoning, isolation of the storage devices on the SAN becomes possible, which is accomplished through FC switches by use of the World Wide Name (WWN).

We can use the Network File System (NTFS) or the Server Message Blocks (SMB) so as to create the network shares.

The opposite of limiting is multipathing. It works by creating multiple paths to our storage devices increasing the fault tolerance as well as the availability.

Network Configurations

The configuration of the network can be done by the use of either Port Address Translation (PAT) or the Network Address Translation (NAT). With NAT, an organization is capable of using only a single address or some set of addresses into the Internet for establishment of computer connections. This means that NAT works by acting as a proxy between a local area network using some private IP addresses and the Internet. NAT is good for hiding your network from the entire world and it will be hard for you to know the systems which are available on the other side of your router.

Although we can use multiple IP addresses (public) in a NAT, in PAT, we can only use one and then share the port with the network. Due to the use of a single IP, Pat is more limited and only good for home-based and other small networks. A good example of PAT implementation is the Internet Connection Sharing for Microsoft.

Subnetting

Subnetting refers to the use of the value for the subnet value so as to divide a network into some smaller components. With this, you will have many networks but each section will have a smaller number of hosts.

The following are the two main reasons as to why we subnet a network:

• to use the IP addresses in a more effective manner,
• to secure the network and make it more manageable.

Supernetting

The CIDR classless inter-domain routing is commonly referred to as supernetting. It works with numerous routing protocols and it groups together numerous networks so as to appear as one. Some of the common routing protocols include:

- RIPv2
- EIGRP
- IS-IS
- BGP
- OSPF
- RIPv1
- IGRP
- EGP

A CIDR block is a block of addresses that makes use of CIDR. With a network of hosts, one may think that there is a physical wire used for interconnecting the hosts, but there exists no such wire. It can help us to contain some traffic on a particular section of the network.

VLAN Tagging

In the case of VLANs which span multiple switches, then the VLAN Tagging will be needed. In this technique, the ID of the VLAN is added to the header of a packet so as to specify the VLAN to which the packet is designated for. The switches will have to consider the VLAN so that it can determine the port through which a packet can be broadcasted through.

The kind of configuration done on the router ports will determine the kind of traffic which is allowed to flow through. You can configure the router so that it can allow in or out individual port traffic, which is referred to as "port forwarding." In case you block a port, no traffic will flow through, and the users may end up suffering.

Network Optimization

This involves the checking of the network measurable and working to improve the numbers. The measurable aspects of the network include bandwidth (for measuring network speed) and latency (which is delay time, either high or low).

Compression refers to the reduction of the size of the data which is to be sent. With caching, data is stored at a location where it can be easily accessed, or closer to home. When devices are kept in the same subnet, optimization will have been improved. This also calls for us to be careful when it comes to the topology:

1. Local Area Network (LAN)- this is a network covering a small space.

2. Metropolitan Area Network (MAN)- this refers to LANs which have been combined in a geographic area.

3. Wide Area Network (WAN)- this is a network made up of multiple LANs/WANs and covering up a very large geographic area.

With load balancing, one is able to distribute their load such as data routing and file requests, meaning that there will be no device which will be overburdened.

Issues with Network Connectivity

Whenever you are testing for network connectivity, there are a number of tools which can help you. These include the following:

1. ping- begin by pinging loopback address, which is 127.0.0.1, followed by the default gateway, and stop at the first sign of trouble so as to figure out what is causing the problem. In case you don't find the issue locally, just go beyond and ping beyond your network.

2. Trace route/tracert- This gives more that the ping as it shows how routes are arranged, thus, allowing one to get from one host to another. It helps you know the path a packet takes to reach the destination.

3. Telnet- this is a tool which allows you to connect to a host located remotely. However, it is not very recommended since it has security issues. This explains why it is blocked at the firewall. The default port for telnet is 23.

4. netstat- this is a tool for showing the network statistics. If you use it without the switches, it will give you the list of all active connections. A **-n** switch shows the active connections and no name resolution will be done while a −b switch shows the executable which was used for creating each of the connections. The −a is the most powerful switch, and it will show "all" the connections which are listening, established, waiting, and others.

5. nslookup/dig- These are the tools which may be used for showing the DNS resolution. After giving an IP address, you will be given the host names, while after giving the host name; the IP address will be reported.

6. ipconfig/ifconfig- These are the tools which shows the IP-related information such as the IP address, the subnet mask, and the default gateway, and other networking related values such as the MAC address. With a /all switch, the display will be expanded further. A /? Gives you all the options which are available.

7. route- This is a tool used for interaction with a routing table and the **route print** displays it. When you give no switches with this command will bring up the list of all options which are possible.

8. arp- we can display the address resolution table or modify it with this tool. There are also options which we can use with it; otherwise, it gives us the list of options which are possible. BY use of the −**a** option, we can view the current entries in the table.

It is good for you to be aware that by the use of system logs, you are able to know what might be happening in your system. Graphical interface tools such as System Log Viewer and Event Viewer can help you to view these. You can also view these by use of command line tools such as cat, tail, grep, and more.

Network Protocols, Topologies and Ports

A port which is tasked with the responsibility of carrying traffic for a particular switch is referred to as a "trunk port." This port usually carries traffic from all the available VLANS. We use this for interconnecting switches to create a network, interconnecting LANs to create a WAN. A fiber optic cable is used for creating such connections, and "access port" is the opposite of such a port.

"Port binding" is responsible for determining if and how the binding of a port can be done. In the case of virtual machines, this can be dynamic, static, or ephemeral. "Port aggregation" refers to the process of combining multiple ports on a particular switch. There are three settings for this namely on, auto, or desirable.

The following are common ports, together with their associated protocols:

- 80 – HTTP
- 443 – HTTPS
- 21 – FTP
- 22 – SSH/SFTP
- 25 – SMTP
- 53 – DNS
- 68 –DHCP/BOOTP
- FTPS – 989 and 990

Types of Networks

Networks can be broken down into three categories which include the following:

- Internet- a network which is open to the world.
- Intranet- a network which is closed to the world.
- Extranet- a network which is only open to some of the world.

Features and Hardware Resources in a Virtual Environment

The BIOS (Basic Input Output System) is responsible for determining what a machine can be able to do. The virtualization of the hardware should be supported by the BIOS, and a firmware update may be needed. The firmware is used for configuration of what the hardware resources such as the hard drive, motherboard, and others are able to do and you need to perform an update on it based on the task you may need to perform.

The following should be noted in the case of the capacity and configuration of the memory:

- The more the better.
- The faster the better.
- It becomes a difficulty to have too much.
- Limits exist on the RAM amount per host recognized by the virtual machine (VMware vs Hyper-V).

During the selection of a CPU, ensure that its architecture is capable of supporting virtualization. One may select processors which have many cores and use more vCPUs compared to the actual number of CPUs cores. Network Interface Cards (NICs) should be chosen based on their speed as well as the configuration speeds that they offer.

Chapter 4- Security

An ACL (**Access Control List**) is more of a guest list. It is used for limiting the system resources or the users who have access and the permissions that they will have after logging in successfully.

Each end of an ACL has a condition referred to as "implicit deny," meaning that if the access or the permission has not been granted up to a point, then it will be denied. The same technology is used in firewalls so as to provide the options given below:

- Block the connection.
- Allow the connection.
- Allow a connection only if it is secured.

In case there is no other condition met, then the default setting is that the connection should be blocked.

Virtual Private Networks- these make use of the Internet for extending a private network. The VPN channel, which runs across the network for practical purposes, seems to be a dedicated channel. Some of the factors which a network administrator must consider when working with VPNs include the following:

- Security
- management policies
- functionality

An **Intrusion Detection System (IDS)** is used when we need to monitor how the network is accessed. The mechanisms are used together with the firewall (software and/or hardware) and then kept inside the firewall for the purpose of monitoring for any intruders. It will monitor your packets and whenever it finds a defect, then a notification about the same will be sent.

An **Intrusion prevention System (IPS)** adds to the function of an IDS by rejecting any packets found with defects. Due to this difference in functionality, an IDS is referred to as a passive system, while the IPS is referred to as an active system. This is because the latter takes an action once a defect is found in the packet.

During the installation process, these two are used together, whereby the IPS is implemented outside the firewall so as to reject any questionable packets which might be trying to get in, while an IDS is implemented inside the firewall so as to look for anything harmful which might have sneaked in.

We can create a **Demilitarized Zone (DMZ)** separately from the LAN/intranet and it is made up of the servers which are visible to the outside world for interaction with it. In most of the cases, this refers to a web server although it is possible for it to be a mail server and other types of servers such as FTP servers. This term and the "perimeter network" are used synonymously, although there might be some differences between the two.

The logs are created by a number of services, and this is determined by the nature of the events. Data is of no use unless one has analyzed it and taken action on it. Administrators should always monitor and analyze the data contained in logs. Type I errors (False positives) and Type II errors (false negatives) greatly prevent the tasks, and they can lead to a false sense of security.

In the case of attacks, the common form of these is the Denial of Service (DoS) attack. In this kind of attack, more traffic will be sent to the server than the amount it is capable of handling. This will mean that the server will not have the capability to handle traffic from legitimate clients. If many computers are involved in this type of attack, this is known as a "Distributed Denial of Service (DDoS) attack."

Security of Storage Devices

Obfusication refers to the technique of masking the data so that it is protected from view by any unauthorized users.

Zoning is a technique used to control access implemented using World Wide Name (WWN) at the hardware level. The WWN are unique identification numbers which are used with SAS, ATA, and Fibre Channel technologies.

Zoning and the Logical Unit Numbering (LUN) are done together, and the latter is implemented at the controller level. Performing the host and user authentication only is not enough for security. That is why you should implement authentication at the level of distinct resources. With this, you will be sure of being secure.

Technologies for Encryption

Let us discuss some of the encryption technologies.

1. Public Key Infrastructure (PKI). This is a means by which we can provide security to transactions and messages in large scale. The PKI technique addresses issues such as support for secure transactions, e-commerce, and privacy of information.

    The PKI helps in creation of trust models, which include hierarchical, bridge, mesh, and hybrid. It is an asymmetric two-key system having four main components which include registration authority (RA), certificate authority (CA), RSA which is the algorithm for encryption, and the digital certificates. Always keep in mind that PKI is a framework, but not a specific technology.

    In this technique, the encryption of messages is done using a public key, while the decryption is done using a private key.

2. IPSec- this is one of the available security protocols which provides a means for authentication and encryption over the Internet. Most network platforms support this, and it is well known for the high level of security it offers. In terms of the OSI model, it works on layer 3. It is highly supported in IPV6 for the creation of VPNs.

    This protocol works together with Layer 2 Forwarding (L2F) or the Layer 2 Tunneling Protocol (L2TP), and the created packets will be hard to be read by a third party. The IPSec uses two primary protocols at the bottom layer, and these include the Encapsulating Security Payload (ESP) and the Authentication Header (AH).

3. Secure Socket Layer (SSL)- this is a protocol which is used when there is a need for one to create some secure connection between two machines which are based on TCP. For a session to be established in this protocol, the basic handshake must be used. Once the client has sent a message to the server requesting a connection, then the server will respond the client by a message stating that a secure connection is needed.

   The client will in turn send a certificate to the server with all the capabilities of the client. The server will in turn evaluate the certificate and then send a response having an encrypted key and a session key. At the end of this process, the session will be more secure.

4. Transport Layer Security (TLS)- this is a security protocol which expands the functionality of the SSL protocol. However, the protocol does not operate together with SSL. The IETF supports the standard for TLS, and many industry analysts have predicted that it will replace SSL. Its default is port 443.

   Ciphers can be placed into two categories, depending on the number of keys which are used. The two categories include:

   - Symmetric ciphers
   - Asymmetric ciphers

   The Symmetric ciphers include the following:

   - Advanced Encryption Standard (AES)- this operates based on the U.S. government agencies with support for keys with sizes 128, 192, and 256 bits. The default bits for this are 128 bits.

- Data Encryption Standard or Triple DES (3DES)- more secure when compared to DES. Its key has a length of 168 bits.

- RC4- this is a WEP/WPA and wireless encryption. It works as a streaming cipher operating with keys of different sizes and used both in TLS and SSL. Most people use this protocol for downloading torrents.

- RC5- this is a block cipher with 2040 bits of key strength.

The asymmetric algorithms include the following:

- Rivest, Shamir and Adleman (RSA)- in which larger integer numbers are used as the basis for the process. Due to its popularity, it has already become a de facto standard. It is based on streams working for both digital signatures and encryption. One can also use RSA for key exchange as well as in SSL.

- Digital Signature Algorithm (DSA)- this is an algorithm which is used for the transmission of digital signatures as well as for exchanging keys. Logarithms are calculated using a block-based method.

The encryption of data can be done either at **Rest** or in **Transit**. The data is said to be at rest when it is in storage, while the data in transit is the one which is being exchanged, hence referred to as "active data."

Identity Access Control Methods

These methods include the following:

1. Role-based Access Control (RBAC)- the access in this model is based on the roles which have been established in the organization. The roles can be based on jobs, responsibility, or even title. If one changes from one role to another, then the access which they had in the previous role will no longer be available.

2. Mandatory Access Control (MAC)- this works differently compared to the RBAC. Due to its inflexibility, it imposes a very rigid model for security. You have to design it very well so that you can enhance the security. The big disadvantage with the access control method is that it lacks flexibility and changes have to be made more frequently. Most government organizations and military use this access control method.

3. Discretionary Access Control (DAC)- in terms of flexibility, the DAC is better than the MAC. The problem with this access control method is that it has an increased risk of disclosing confidential information. A good example of this is the permission system in Unix/Linux, whereby we have the owner and the group based on roles.

In the case of multi-factor authentication, the authentication factors depend on the following values:

- Something that you are.
- Something that you have.
- Something that you know.
- Somewhere that you are.
- Something that you do.

The identification is done using biometrics, username, or Personal Identification Verification Card.

4. Single Sign-On- this is enabled by technologies such as Microsoft Active Directory, Kerberos, Novell eDirectory, and others.

5. Federated Identity- this refers to the linking of electronic identities of an individual across multiple systems for identity management. Layer 7 and ping identity are some of the examples of the cloud integration federation offerings, and these make a number of cloud resources to be available by the use of a single username and password. This helps us to extend the Active Directory to the cloud.

Guest and Host Hardening Techniques

For one to harden their network, they have to pay attention to each aspect of the network, including the servers, workstations, and others. The **attack surface** is the area which is accessible or available to the users, included both the authenticated and the un-authenticated users. The attack surface can be made up of protocols, services, code, and interfaces.

A smaller attack surface means that there is a less likelihood that there will be an attack. If the attack surface is too large, there is more likelihood that the surface will be targeted. An **attack surface reduction (ASR)** aims at minimizing the possibility of exploitation by reduction of the attack surface and a limit on the potential damage.

To limit the potential damage, you have to turn off some of the unnecessary functions, limit entry points, reduce privileges, and add some authentication requirements. Any unneeded ports and services should be disabled. Accounts which are no longer needed should be deleted or deactivated, default passwords changed, and the default accounts deactivated. Antivirus software programs as well as other antimalware programs should be kept up to date with patches installed after they have been tested on non-production machines. This will help in the minimization of zero-day exploits.

In the case of security and hardening, you should let your common sense guide you in all actions you take to ensure that these are implemented.

Chapter 5- Systems Management

Policies and Procedures

In the case of network and IP planning, you have to do it carefully, and it will never satisfy you, meaning that you will keep on tweaking it. It is good for you to have a back-up plan, and monitoring and documentation after each tweak is of great importance.

During the documentation process, you should put it in mind that you will not be the network administrator forever, in that someone else may come and need to make use of the documentation so as to understand the layout of the network before making any changes which might be needed.

The best practices for change management expect you to create documentation which is usable. Some level of approval process and configuration control is expected, and this should implement an effective approval process. Asset accountability is also very essential.

To make configuration standardized, you should use a Change Manager or a Change Team, or choose to combine both. It will be good for all the stakeholders to be consulted before a change can be made.

To automate the configuration management, one can make use of **CMDB (Configuration Management Database).** This will help you with the configuration control and approval process and help you with the process of documentation.

Capacity Management is the process of monitoring for any changes which are made, and look so as to see what is trending. The windows for maintenance should be identified and then used for making upgrades to the server and patch installation for the purpose of minimizing service interruptions and downtime as much as we can.

The **Systems Life Cycle Management Tools** provides us with structure and guidelines for the operations. Examples of such tools include the Information Technology Infrastructure Library (ITIL) and the Microsoft Operations Framework (MOF). The MOF can be broken further into the following four components:

- Plan
- Deliver
- Operate
- Manage

According to Microsoft, the MOF is classified as a solutions accelerator and to use it, make sure that you download its latest version.

Optimizing Performance of Physical Host

Each administrator needs to get the best performance possible from the system. Some of the key areas of measurement of performance include the following:

1. Disk Performance- this can be improved through caching and indexing. Some of the key metrics which you should watch include the number of metrics and throughput.

2. Disk tuning- defragmentation can help in reducing the load times for files, but this will apply only if the drives are in the form of hard drives as opposed to solid drives. Some of the important metrics which you should watch and tweak include the controller-related variables and block sizes.

3. Disk latency- for you to monitor this, you have to watch for average response time.

4. Swap disk space- the performance associated with a single file usually improves with contiguous data; nowhere is this case more than with swap file/space which has been used. That is why you should set aside some space so as to allow for growth without having to use different locations.

5. I/O tuning- SQLIO, which is a tool designed to be used with the SQL server can be used for determination of the I/O capacity for a particular configuration, and the tool has been developed by Microsoft. With the tool, it will be easy for you to alter the size of the I/O request.

A number of tools exist for performance monitoring and management.

Performance logs and alerts

These are the WMI (Windows Management and Instrumentation) objects. The sets to be monitored include the VirtualNetwork counters SAR (to monitor the system activity), VirtualMachine counters, and STRACE (for system calls/signals). For all the tools that you use, your aim should be to eliminate any bottlenecks and make documentation on anything that you do. The more of everything that you use, that is, RAM, processor and hard disk space, the better. Any changes made to the virtual environment should be carefully watched to establish any effects and thwart any problems which might occur. Some of the problems which may occur in the virtual environment include the following:

- Disk Failure
- HBA Failure
- Memory Failure
- NIC Failure
- CPU Failure

Performance Concepts

The input/output operations per second (IOPS) is a de facto standard which is used for the purpose of measuring the disk performance. The two main forms of disk operations are **reading** and **writing,** and both of these operations can be optimized.

The file systems are proprietary and they have something which they can offer to the market. It is good for you to decide on the file system which you should use based on your requirement and then look for ways to optimize its performance.

Caching can be achieved by the use of RAM as well as other microcontrollers. When this is implemented using controllers, the writes will be delayed, which might leave you at risk whenever a crash of the system happens, but it is good in speeding the rate of read operations by reading ahead per operation.

Bandwidth may be a bottleneck since the performance is highly dependent on it. To increase **throughput,** you may choose to aggregate a number of resources so that they may appear as one, by the use of **teaming** or **bonding.** Jumbo frames are large Ethernet frames, and if you send many of these, they will not be processor intensive.

The focus of **Network Latency** is on delays. This can be tested by use of a tool such as PRTG's Network Latency Test.

Hop count is used for determining the number of stops that will be done on a route, and it can be determined by use of tracert.

Quality of service (QoS) is used for identification and prioritization of data, and this becomes very useful when it comes to load balancing by use of a load balancer. Multipathing is used to create multiple and redundant routes. Scaling can be implemented vertically, horizontally, or diagonally.

Vertical scaling can also be referred to as scaling up, and it involves the addition of resources to a particular node. The resources added can be the processor, memory, and others. Horizontal scaling can also be referred to as scaling out, and it involves the addition of more nodes. Diagonal scaling involves the combination of these two types of scaling.

Testing Techniques

The techniques of testing are based on what you need to test. Some of the factors which you may need to test include latency, bandwidth, load balancing, storage, etc.

You should do a **vulnerability test** so as to determine and know the weaknesses before the others can do this. This is mostly done by use of a vulnerability scanner, which is a software application which works by checking your network for any holes applications and the computer themselves. Examples of common vulnerability scanners include the following:

- Nessus
- Retina
- SAINT and OpenVAS

Errors and frauds during testing can be prevented by implementing the separation of duties (SoD).

Chapter 6- Business Continuity in the Cloud

Disaster Recovery Methods and Concepts

You should look for means of implementing redundancy for each component you have in the cloud. **Failover** refers to the process of switching to the redundant system once a failure has occurred.

Failback means that an alternative plan can be used in case of an emergency. With **site mirroring,** one will be allowed to have another location which you can use in case this one is destroyed, and the location can be classified as hot, warm, or cold.

A **hot site** refers to a site which can provide operations hours after a failure has occurred. This calls for the site to have servers, telecommunication equipment, and networks so as to ensure that it can provide services for a few hours after a failure has occurred.

The network connections can help to ensure that the databases are kept up-to-date. The systems are very expensive, and they are the best ones in the case of short term situations. An hot site may also work as an offsite storage facility, and it will provide for immediate access to backup media and archives. A hot site is also given the name **active backup model.**

A **warm site** is capable of providing some of the capabilities of the hot site, but the user is required to do a lot so as to make the site operational. They usually offer computer systems as well as compatible media capabilities. If this kind of site is being used, then the administrators will have to install and then configure systems so that operations can be resumed.

A **cold site** refers to a facility which is not ready to be used. The organization which needs to use this must come with their network as well as other equipment. Although it may provide the network, this is not the case, as it should only provide a place for the operations to be resumed, but no infrastructure to support the operations.

The main disadvantage with cold sites is that the user has to do lot of work so as to be able to resume operations. They are the least expensive when it comes to setting them up, but one should do good planning and testing for it to be fully operational.

The cold sites usually work well after an anticipation of extended outage. However, the consumer should be ready to provide all the facilities which are necessary for the site to be operational.

Solid documentation is of importance if you need to have an effective site. If the redundant systems are in separate geographical regions, one will be able to access their data in case a disaster occurs in one part of the country.

The following are some of the acronyms which are associated with recovery and redundancy:

- RTO- Recovery Time Objectives
- RPO- Recovery Point Objective
- MTBF- Mean Time Between Failure
- MTTR- Mean Time To Recovery
- MTTF- Mean Time to Failure

Availability Requirements

The aim of implementing fault tolerance is to achieve availability. Local geoclustering/clustering is a way which can help us to achieve this. Remember that implementing fault tolerance on the hardware level alone is not enough. This is why you should ensure that there is no single point of failure (SPoF) in your system. Multiple paths should be used for the provision of connectivity and ensuring that there is redundancy.

Load balancing helps us to distribute our load across multiple systems so as to avoid issues with the loading of a single server.

Conclusion

We have come to the end of the book. Those are the topics which are covered in the CompTIA Cloud+ exam (CV0-001). This book has explored them in detail, and in a way that is easy for anyone to understand. Focus on the details which we have discussed and you will pass the exam!

www.ingramcontent.com/pod-product-compliance
Lightning Source LLC
Chambersburg PA
CBHW061032050326
40689CB00012B/2786